# Celebrating Birthdays
# in China

by Cheryl L. Enderlein

**Content Consultant**

Verna Tang
Reference Librarian
Chinese Information and Culture Center

# Bridgestone Books
an imprint of Capstone Press
Mankato, Minnesota

Bridgestone Books are published by Capstone Press
151 Good Counsel Drive, P.O. Box 669, Mankato, Minnesota 56002
http://www.capstone-press.com

*Library of Congress Cataloging-in-Publication Data*
Enderlein, Cheryl L.
    Celebrating birthdays in China/by Cheryl L. Enderlein.
    p. cm.--(Birthdays around the world)
    Includes bibliographical references (p. 23) and index.
    Summary: Discusses the parties, decorations, food, music, games, and presents
found at Chinese birthday celebrations.
    ISBN 1-56065-761-8
    1. Birthdays--Juvenile literature.  2. Children's parties--China--Juvenile literature.
3. China--Social life and customs--Juvenile literature. [1. Birthdays. 2. Parties.
3. China--Social life and customs.] I. Title. II. Series.
    GV1472.7.B5E526   1998
    394.2--dc21
                                                                97-44679
                                                                    CIP
                                                                    AC

**Editorial credits**

Editor, Mark Drew; additional editing, Colleen Sexton; cover design, Timothy Halldin;
    photo research, Michelle L. Norstad

**Photo credits**

Argus Photoland, LTD., 6, 8, 12, 16, 20; Shinichi Ishikawa, 10
Image Bank/Guang Jui Xie, 14
Christopher Liu, cover, 18
Unicorn Stock Photos/Jeff Greenberg, 4

2  3  4  5  6  06  05  04  03  02  01

# Table of Contents

## 樹下誕生

本行經云摩耶聖母懷孕將滿十月垂
嵐毘尼園大吉祥地安詳徐步慶處觀
波羅义柔軟低垂夫人即舉右手攀彼
光明即時諸天世間悉皆遍照時天帝
衣裹於自手承接太子。

戊辰春欲月陳羲

四明一九㐅書圓聯供句弁書

# Facts about China

China is located in eastern Asia. It is the third largest country in the world. Only Russia and Canada are bigger than China.

China has many different kinds of land. The land in eastern China is flat. Mountains cover western China. Deserts stretch across the north.

China has more people than any other country. About one-fifth of the world's people live in China. One-fifth means one out of every five people.

People from China are called Chinese. The language they speak is also called Chinese. There are many different kinds of Chinese. But most people speak a kind of Chinese called Mandarin.

The Chinese language has no alphabet. Each word is made of one sign instead of several letters. But some signs stand for many words in Chinese.

**Each word is a sign in the Chinese language.**

# What Is a Birthday?

A birthday is the day a person was born. Each person has a birthday once every year.

In China, a person's year of birth is also important. Chinese people have a special calendar that covers 12 years. Each year is named after an animal. The year 1997 was the year of the Ox. The first six years are Rat, Ox, Tiger, Rabbit, Dragon, and Snake. The next six years are Horse, Sheep, Monkey, Rooster, Dog, and Pig. The calendar starts over every 12 years.

Each person has an animal sign. It is the sign of the year when the person was born. Some Chinese believe the sign tells what the person is like. They also believe the animal sign tells the person's future.

The special calendar is one tradition in China. A tradition is something people have done for many years.

Each year in the Chinese calendar is named after an animal.

# Family Parties

Chinese people celebrate when a person turns one year older. Celebrate means to do something fun on a special occasion. Chinese people have family birthday parties. This means the parties are for both adults and children.

Grandparents, aunts, uncles, and cousins come to the parties. Chinese people also invite friends. Invite means to ask people to come.

The family of the birthday person gives the party. Family members prepare for the party for many days. Some family members clean the house. Others cook special foods for the birthday person.

People buy the birthday person new clothes or shoes. This is another tradition in China. It is important for the birthday person to wear new things. It shows that a new year of life has begun.

Chinese people have family birthday parties.

# Birthday Noodles and Peach

Chinese people eat long noodles on their birthdays. This is another tradition. The long noodles stand for long life. Many Chinese people believe eating these noodles brings good luck.

Many Chinese people eat with chopsticks. Chopsticks are two thin pieces of wood. They are about 8 inches (20 centimeters) long. The Chinese hold the chopsticks in one hand.

People in China do not eat many sweet things. They may have a birthday peach instead of a birthday cake.

In China, a birthday peach is a steamed dumpling. Birthday peaches are made of flour and water. They are a little bit sweet.

Sometimes the cook puts a red dot on a peach. The red dot stands for good luck. Sometimes the cook puts a surprise inside the birthday peach. The surprise might be coins.

**Chinese people eat long noodles on their birthdays.**

# Presents

People who come to a birthday party are called guests. Adult guests bring presents to the birthday person.

Guests often bring money. They fold paper money and tuck it into a small, red envelope. The envelope is red for good luck. Chinese people call this gift a red bag.

Jade is a common gift for babies. Jade is a green stone. In China, some people believe that jade keeps a person safe.

The stone has a symbol cut into it. A symbol is an object that stands for something else. People pick symbols that stand for long life or good luck. Chinese people give jade to babies to wish them a long life.

**Guests put money in a small red envelope.**

# A Chinese Feast

A big Chinese meal is called a feast. Chinese people serve a feast during a special birthday party.

A feast has 12 main dishes. The first four dishes are cold salads. The next four dishes are stir fry. Stir fry is meat or vegetables cooked quickly over high heat. One kind of stir fry is cooked vegetables in sauce.

The last four foods are stews. Stews are foods that cook for a long time. They usually include meat. Chinese people eat soup between stir fry and stews. They also eat rice or noodles with the meal.

Chinese people serve the food family style. They place each dish in a big bowl. People pass the bowls around the table. They eat a little of each dish.

**A Chinese birthday feast has 12 main dishes.**

# First Year of Life

Chinese people believe the first year of life is unsafe. In the past, babies often got sick. Sometimes a baby did not live through its first year.

Chinese people celebrate twice after a baby is born. Family members celebrate when a baby is one month old. They also celebrate when a baby turns one year old. The family believes the baby is now out of danger. They are happy that the child is healthy.

The family has a party on each of these important dates. Family members serve a feast. Guests come to help celebrate.

The guests eat long noodles and boiled eggs at the feast. The egg shells are dyed red for good luck. The eggs are also symbols of long life. Giving red eggs means wishing a child a long life.

**Family members celebrate when a child turns one year old.**

# Turning 61

Chinese people respect older people. They believe older people are wise. The oldest person in a family is the most important. Birthdays become more important as a person ages.

Chinese people believe old age begins at 40 years old. They believe old age ends at 60 years old. At 61, a person begins a new life. Families celebrate this important day. They have a big party and a feast.

The birthday person dresses in new clothes for the party. He or she sits at the head of a special table. Sometimes the table is covered with a red table cloth.

Family members bow to the birthday person to show their respect. Guests often give money or gold as presents.

In China, birthdays become more important as a person ages.

# Chinese New Year

Long ago, Chinese people did not celebrate their own birthdays. Instead, they celebrated the birthdays of their leaders. They also celebrated Chinese New Year. This was a birthday party for all Chinese people.

Today, Chinese New Year is a time to welcome the new year. Everyone celebrates the new year together. The celebration can last for several days. People wear new clothes. Friends and families visit each other. They give each other presents.

Families gather for a big meal on New Year's Eve. They set off fireworks at midnight. Some Chinese people believe the fireworks scare away evil spirits. Some people wear dragon costumes and dance. The dragon is a symbol of good luck.

**Chinese people set off fireworks at midnight on New Year's Eve.**

# Hands On: Make Red Eggs

Many Chinese people believe red eggs bring good luck. You can make your own red eggs.

## What You Need

6 eggs
Pot with cover
Water
Bowl
1/2 teaspoon red food coloring

2 teaspoons vinegar
2 cups of hot water
Spoon
Paper towel

## What You Do

1. Put the eggs in the pot. Fill the pot with enough water to cover the eggs.
2. Place the pot on a stove. Ask an adult to turn on the burner. Wait until the water boils. Be careful! The stove and water are hot!
3. Ask and adult to cover the pot and turn off the burner. Let the eggs sit for 30 minutes. Ask the adult to pour out the water.
4. Put the food coloring, vinegar, and hot water into the bowl. Stir.
5. Use the spoon to put the eggs into the bowl. Take out the eggs when they turn red.
6. Put the eggs on a paper towel to dry. Serve them when they are cool.

## Words to Know

**celebrate** (SEHL-uh-brayt)—to do something fun on a special occasion

**chopsticks** (CHOP-stihks)—two thin pieces of wood used to eat

**guest** (GEST)—a person who comes to a party

**invite** (in-VITE)—to ask people to come

**Mandarin** (MAN-dur-in)—the kind of Chinese spoken by most Chinese people

**peach** (PEECH)—a sweet dumpling

**tradition** (truh-DISH-uhn)—something people have done for many years

## Read More

**Dahl, Michael**. *China*. Countries of the World. Mankato, Minn.: Bridgestone Books, 1998.

**Dawson, Zoë**. *China*. Austin, Tex.: Raintree Steck-Vaughn, 1996.

**Feldman, Eve B**. *Birthdays! Celebrating Life Around the World*. Mahwah, N.J.: BridgeWater Books, 1996.

**Flint, David**. *China*. On the Map. Austin, Tex.: Raintree Steck-Vaughn, 1994.

## Useful Addresses

**China Institute in America**
125 E. 65th Street
New York, NY 10021

**Chinese Information and
 Culture Center**
1230 Avenue of the Americas
New York, NY 10020-1513

## Internet Sites

**Kids Parties Connection**
http://kidsparties.com

**Zoom School: China**
http://www.enchantedlearning.com/school/China

## Index